Straw Men, Paper Tigers & Puppets:

The Philosophy of Knowns and Unknowns

Dr. Ray C. Minor

RoseDog Books
PITTSBURGH, PENNSYLVANIA 15238

RoseDog Books
585 Alpha Drive, Suite 103
Pittsburgh, PA 15238
Visit our website at www.rosedogbookstore.com

ISBN: 978-1-6470-2396-6
eISBN: 978-1-6470-2149-8

Contents

Introduction

In order to provide a sense of who I am, I provide a biographical sketch of my life up front entitled "Growing up in Cottondale". The title Straw Men, Paper Tigers & Puppets suggests that life is not ideal and no person, place or thing is perfect. It also implies that life is theatrical and everyone plays a role. Being young is the best of human existence. It is an awakening period where we make life long decisions about who we are and where we belong. Arguably, it is the most determinative period of our lives.

I believe that life is more meaningful than survival. Life begins when you find a purpose. It ends when that purpose is complete. Your experiences will follow you into eternity. Life is what you create. You must maintain a healthy outlook on life and know that a brighter tomorrow is ahead. With hope comes the courage to pickup your burdens and carry on with life. Without hope you lose your will to live, your desire to achieve, your capacity to love, your ability to cope, your sense of belonging, and your quest for peace.

Why do some people succeed and others do not? I believe that mental attitude is a determining factor in whether you succeed or fail. A person succeeds because he chooses a goal that is attainable and follows a course of action that leads to the goal. Failure is a stumbling block that can be overcome through knowledge, skill, experience, time and ability.

I believe that philosophy is a leisure exploration of the mind fueled by outside stimuli. It is a quest to understand the unknown universe. It is discovering and conceptualizing the unknown for the purposes of advancing civilization and enjoyment of human life.

Politics is about compromise and politicians are swayed by special interests. Politics is a contact sport. There are winners and losers, and rewards and punishments. Politics is the power to control, influence and manipulate human and material resources. Politics is about decision-making and the allocation of resources.

This book is about the challenges, hopes and dreams that people grapple with everyday. It is a book of rich thoughts on being young, spirituality, hope, success, philosophy and politics. It is rife with common sense and inspiration.

Growing Up in Cottondale

I grew up in a rural blue-collar community called Cottondale (now incorporated into the City of Tuscaloosa) in the 1950s and 60s. My mother was reared by her grandparents as her mother passed away when she was age six; and my father was reared by a white family in the 1930s and 40s in Cottondale after he was declared a ward of the court at age six. However, Cottondale was segregated during this time. The Black enclave of Cottondale settled there shortly after slavery. It was a community situated on the east side of Tuscaloosa, Alabama. My community was comprised of approximately 30 anchor families. The geography of the community was hilly, heavily vegetated with pine, cedar, oak and occasional pecan, mulberry, apple, walnut, chinaberry, persimmon, cherry and hickory nut trees. The roadways were dirt and gravel buttressed by a state highway and a railroad. The main road looped around the community in the shape of a horseshoe. The railroad separated the white blue-collar community from my community. Further, at the crest of the horseshoe was a middleclass white community separated by forest. Both white communities had paved streets. There was very little interaction among the communities.

There was a small grocery store and a fruit stand located in the white blue-collar neighborhood that served the communities. There was also a concrete pipe company and lumberyard that employed some of the neighbors. Others were employed outside the community as maids and servants or as laborers at a steel plant, paper mill or rubber plant or as orderlies, aides and custodial workers and laborers for private homes and major institutions. None of the family members were college educated prior to my generation. Most of the family members had some high school education but few were high school graduates. Some of the men were military veterans of WWII, Korean and Vietnam wars. Oddly though the community placed value on education. Generally, the neighbors appeared to have good common sense, cherished the work ethic, and praised God. The spirit of the community was situated in a Baptist church. Later, a Church of God was established but attracted very little attendance and closed after a short period of operation. What is important and relevant about my growing up in segregated Tuscaloosa is that the Black community and culture instilled a sense of pride and dignity that my life was meaningful. It also inculcated hope that I too could attain the "American dream" if I worked hard enough. Although the community was apolitical in the sense it was not organizing or engaging neighbors in major public issues, though a few did, it was keenly aware of the social movements and the terrorist groups and forces fighting change.

Neighbors appeared to be attentive to the media. I mean many neighbors read newspapers, watched television and listen to radio broadcasts. Some would discuss political maters or current events as they visited the homes of one another. The majority of households operated by the "open door" policy. Any neighbor was welcomed in another's home without notice at any time. Generally, the neighbors knew how to avoid wearing out that welcome. The neighbors shared resources whether it was a cup of sugar, fresh vegetables from the garden, a lawn tool or a pail of water. For those not familiar, back then most unincorporated areas utilized wells (that tapped into a water table) as water sources for drinking, cooking, washing and bathing. My family had a well on their property and any neighbor could draw from it. These customs strengthen the bonds of community-largely unspoken.

It was the right thing to do. This phenomenon was a custom that was passed down from one generation to the next.

Most of the families were large with some having 12 or more children. I am from a family of 9 siblings. Albeit, this situation meant that the warm months were very lively as children were playing football, baseball or softball on a designated "community field"; or basketball wherever there was something resembling a basketball hoop (in some cases a bicycle rim nailed to a tree or a basketball goal without nets nailed to a tree). Boys and girls played hopscotch, jump rope, hula hoops, jacks and marbles. Barbecue and chitterlings filled the air on the Fourth of July. Someone in the community would roast a pig. Mostly though the menu was barbeque ribs and chicken with sides of greens, corn, baked beans, mac and cheese, coleslaw, sweet potato pie, pecan pie, and homemade ice cream. These backyard cookouts generated a festive scene. Thanksgivings were very festive too and served as family reunions.

Half of the families had two heads of household and at least one working during the week. Usually, the adults shopped on Saturday and the families attended church on Sunday. I must admit that church services including preaching were taxing on the children. The adults also socialized on Friday and Saturday nights. There were several "shot houses" and "Juke Joints" in the community. Even though there was a white elementary school in walking distance from my home, school aged children in my community were bused to segregated black schools five or more miles away. For some black children in my community this status did not change until 1969 and for others in 1970 in spite of the Brown Decision in 1954. So I attended segregated schools until my senior year 1970. My mother and others spoke about a one room schoolhouse located in my community that provided education prior to my birth. So, after 1970, children of my community were bused to desegregated schools five miles away and some walked to the former white elementary school in the area.

Initially, this desegregated experience placed the adults (parents, teachers and school administrators) on edge as they feared for the safety of the students. The students got along very well and nothing extraordinary happened to endanger a child or disrupt the schools. Although I was occasionally on the honor roll at the Black high school, I was placed in an 11th grade homeroom at the white high school during my senior year. The explanation given was that I did not have enough academic credits to sit in a 12th grade homeroom. So everyday after roll call I went to my senior classes. If I had completed my senior year at the Black high school, I could have finished up by lunch each school day and worked the afternoons. Any way, I was told that I needed to take seven classes. There were only seven periods in a school day. So, that meant that I would have classes all day without break except for lunch. Therefore, I enrolled for seven classes. I graduated with roughly 300 of my classmates on time in 1971.

There were two incidents at the high school worth mentioning. The principal was somewhat of a drill sergeant and his wife was on staff as a counselor. One of her roles as counselor was to walk around with a six-inch rule and measure the distance between the hem of a girl's dress and her knee. If the dress was too short the girl would be ordered to change into appropriate attire. James Brown had just released a popular recording that year titled "Super Bad" and a line in the lyrics was "I got soul and I'm super bad". So, I hand printed that line on a white t-shirt and wore it too school. I wasn't making a political statement and didn't think much of it until the principal sent a student aide to my classroom and summoned me to his office. The principal scolded me that I may have a soul but he did not think I was super bad. He ordered me to go home and change shirts. The student aide took me home and I changed shirts. I arrived back at the school and all was calm.

Overall, the desegregated educational experience was an eye opening one for me. Many myths about intelligence and race were destroyed. I learned that race did not make a difference in matters related to intelligence. In my case, the two races (Back and White) spanned the intelligence scale. I also learned that "boys" will be "boys" and "girls" will be "girls". I learned too that the fears of adults to educational desegregation were more imaginary than real. The bottom line was that human beings tended to fear the unknown and they were more comfortable in their own subculture that shared their customs, norms, beliefs and behaviors.

At some point during my senior year I decided not to attend college until after a three-year break. It worked out that after a three-year break and without doing anything academic, I took the ACT and applied to the University of Alabama. I scored poorly on the ACT. Incidentally, I met my future wife during that time who was already enrolled at the university. So, an admission counselor at the University advised me to attend a local community college for a quarter to prove I could cut it. I did and made "As" and "Bs". I went back to the counselor and her response was ok, do one more quarter. I shook my head and enrolled again at the community college and made "As and "Bs". I went back to the counselor and informed her of my transcript of "As" and "Bs". The counselor suggested that I complete one more quarter at the community college and if successful I could then transfer to the University as a sophomore. So, I did and completed a bachelor's degree at the University in approximately two years. I worked my way through school and took full advantage of the federal aid that was available to me. I also became a student leader.

As I reflect back on my community, there are some important lessons I take away. This segregated community instilled in me a sense of pride, hope and belonging. At any given time, three or four generations of Blacks lived in the community. Everyone was in the same social class (working class poor). There were strong bonds and ties among neighbors. There were examples of exemplary character. There existed a sense of pride in independence and ownership of property. I recall my mother lamenting over welfare benefits. After divorcing my father in 1965 she was placed on welfare, a status she detested. She desired to earn her living and took herself off the welfare rolls within a year.

The vast majority of families owned their homes and land. I believe that most inherited their homesteads. Most neighbors communicated with one another on a regular basis. Therefore, each neighbor knew the struggles of the other. The community instilled a sense of identity even though not formal. Somehow and perhaps through experience neighbors knew the importance of being Black and the dangers of living in the segregated South. Without verbalizing it, Black consciousness and identity were transmitted through their being. All children in the community lived the Black experience through their families, neighbors, churches and schools. They identified as Black and offered no misgivings about that identity either.

Being Young

Being young, healthy, active and inquisitive is the best of human existence. So, what should be done to prepare for a rewarding future? It is a simple thing to comprehend but perhaps one of the most challenging things in our lives. However, it is something we all must confront. While young we have the freedom to chart our future. We determine our destinies by what we believe, what choices we make, how we behave, what we learn, what we eat and how we exercise.

The important decisions we make today will define our tomorrow. We may choose to live a productive life. We may decide to live a destructive one. Or, like many we may choose to be a little bit productive and a little bit destructive. Just lounging in between the two. It is really up to us. We have free will. It is our lives. The choices are ours. While in our youth, we develop character, personality, belief system, social, personal and political identities and moral compass. In essence, we are preparing for adulthood. We become introspective about who we are and where we belong in society. It is a period of decision making. A period of change and uncertainty. It is one of the most pivotal points in our lives.

Typically, life is like a jungle. You may have heard people say so. Life is complex and confusing and often we have to fend for ourselves. As though we live in a world where only the strong survives. In the words of Darwin, it is a world of survival of the fittest. While these things may be true, the jungle metaphor may be true as well. The world is full of mysteries and challenges. Full of untamed innocence and adventure. However, as with any jungle, the jungle of life can be conquered.

- ❖ You must possess the right tools, knowledge and skills.
- ❖ You must learn all there is while the gifts of youth, health and strength are at your disposal.
- ❖ You must dream today about what you would like to become in life.
- ❖ You must take life seriously. Life is real. Life is not a music video featuring Beyonce or Jay Z. Nor is it a slam dunk by Michael Jordan or LeBron James.
- ❖ You must learn to organize your time. You must know when to work and play.
- ❖ You must be open and honest with yourself. Know who you are and your limitations.
- ❖ You must realize your potential.
- ❖ You must not be afraid to face new challenges.
- ❖ You must understand the society in which you live.
- ❖ You must participate fully in society.
- ❖ You must express love and understanding for yourself and humankind.
- ❖ You must drink from the well of moral authority. Always favor good over evil.
- ❖ You must master life and all of its wonders and opportunities.
- ❖ You must realize that your life is timed and live every minute to its fullness.
- ❖ You must understand that to live the good life requires mastering reading, writing, language, math and technology.
- ❖ You must have a plan of action.
- ❖ You must practice self-control and self-discipline.
- ❖ You are indebted to yourself, your family and society to do the best that you can with every task you undertake.

❖ You must understand that it is not so important where you were born, or to whom you were born, or what you appear to be. It does not matter whether you have rags or riches. It matters most where you end up.

Journey of Life

God is a greater force or being penetrating and guiding our minds toward justice; interwoven into the fabric of our subconscious minds; and forms our thoughts and actions. God is a true companion in time of need and despair; possesses the answer to everything; has no boundaries. God covers the universe.

Human beings have a mission on earth. It goes beyond mere love for humankind. It is greater than the structures that stand in major cities. It propels faster than the rockets that soar through time and space. It dwells deeper than the oceans and seas that fill the cavities of the earth. It steeps higher than the mountains that peak across the roughed terrain. It is all these things and more.

Time is constant. We are energized through the golden rays of sunshine. We mature in the falling drops of rain. Life is more meaningful than survival. We trek through life in search of purpose. Life begins when we find that purpose. It ends when the purpose is complete.

Life on earth will follow us into eternity. There is more to life than just living. There is meaning to all of the mundane and frivolous things that prey upon our time and energy. We are more meaningful than our mere existence. It goes beyond helping one another. There is something after life. Life is what we create. Our mission in life is to find meaning. Life is more than the appearance of things. Our journey eagerly awaits us.

- ❖ If our goal in life is to please ourselves, we have already failed. If our goal is to please others, we will become gravely disappointed. But if our goal is to please God, we will be richly rewarded.
- ❖ Today, we have a chance to achieve or move closer to our goal which may mean moving closer to our God. If the ultimate goal in life is to move closer to God then what does an earthly goal mean?
- ❖ God is an unfolding pathway of truth.
- ❖ God moves through every just cause.
- ❖ The best way to help others is to teach them to help themselves.
- ❖ Faith is the door to the future.
- ❖ A person's religion is her prerogative.
- ❖ Religion should open minds not close them.
- ❖ Faith is the basis of confidence.
- ❖ Confidence is the foundation of courage.
- ❖ If we travel the straight and narrow road prepare for ostracism and stoning.
- ❖ Why do people create their own hell?
- ❖ An evil soul must be a painful burden.
- ❖ If there is a good spirit in us, nurture it so it may protect us from the evil one.
- ❖ The church is an empty vessel without the souls of the people.
- ❖ If there is justice, the evil we do will be recompensed.
- ❖ How many prayers will tame a wicked spirit?
- ❖ We are the angels we seek. Be the angels we seek.
- ❖ Recognize angels in our lives. These are the people who show kindness and goodness.
- ❖ Be forever faithful.
- ❖ Reading is rewarding. It helps us put together the puzzles of life.

- ❖ The secrets of life come through revelation and realization.
- ❖ Turning points signal change. These are times to reflect and refocus on life's mission-the reason why you are here. Time-out so to speak. Are you traveling on the right track? Should you be doing something else? These are questions to focus on to find your way to your original purpose. Life is short. So, every day not purpose driven is a precious waste of time.
- ❖ Life is a challenge. You must take advantage of chances.
- ❖ Your station in life lies upon your shoulders.
- ❖ Life is too brief and valuable to spend on misery.
- ❖ Life is too short to count every penny.
- ❖ A full life is daring.
- ❖ Life is a universal game that everyone must play.
- ❖ Do what you must in life then life will not be in vain.
- ❖ What is the value of a poor life? Is a rich life better? What about a good life?
- ❖ Our goal in life should not be to have people admire us but to have them realize the value of our lives.
- ❖ Life is strange. People respond more readily to the appearance of things.

Rays of Hope

If you are depressed, down and out, broke, homeless, helpless, lonely, troubled and without sunshine in your life, what will do you have to live? You must learn early in life to expect dark clouds sometimes to hover over your playground. You must realize that it is not wise to play in a storm. You should know that natural fires burn in the forest to maintain the natural order of things. You should also learn that bad news travels the same streets as good news. You must know that accidents do occur and young people die as well as older ones.

However, you should realize too that dark clouds do not last forever. You must be mindful that a brilliant rainbow appears after the storm. You must not become too preoccupied with your current situation that you fail to plan for a better future. You must maintain a healthy outlook on life and know that a brighter tomorrow is ahead. You should remember those sunny days of the past while you travel through the cloudy days of the present. This is what gives you hope that everything will work out just fine. With this hope comes the courage to pickup your burdens and carry on with life. Hope gives back your will to live.

With this hope you are able to dream of a better day where your condition will not be windy and stormy, but calm and sunny. Hope is the key to keeping your mental sky sunny and blue. With hope you can weather the storms of life. Without hope you lose your will to live, your desire to achieve, your capacity to love, your ability to cope, your sense of belonging, and your quest for peace. It is your ray of inspiration.

- Today is a time in which every day may be the last.
- There is nothing greater than being oneself.
- Greatness always prevails.
- Do not allow your self-concept or self-esteem to become tainted, eroded, contaminated or devalued.
- If you want to be great free yourself from selfishness.
- Have confidence in the day. Everything will be okay.
- Create opportunities and take advantage of them while time is on your side.
- If you are going somewhere take a purpose with you.
- Never take criticism personally. Use it as a learning opportunity. It will help you grow.
- Your end is not where you are standing today. Your end is where you are when all is said and done.
- Peace for today is hope for tomorrow.
- You are where you are for a reason; find the reason.
- If you are tired of taking orders, become independent and call the shots.
- The things that concern you the most are not found on the mountaintops but most likely on the plains.
- If you knew better, would you do better?
- The first 15 days and last 15 days of the year would be better spent in meditation and hibernation.
- Why not begin the New Year by filling your schedule with the right things?
- The New Year is yours to control. You are in charge.
- The New Year is yours. Grab it by the tail.
- If you knew the truth, how would your outlook change? How would you adjust your mindset and goals?

- ❖ Do things that make you grow.
- ❖ You are your inner voice.
- ❖ Have a belly full of laughter today!
- ❖ If you are always looking downward, how will you be able to see things above and beyond?
- ❖ Learn to burn off misery and shame.
- ❖ If you are bound by good principles, how could you be lead astray?
- ❖ Why rush? We can never overcome time.
- ❖ No one is born to lose. Everyone has a chance to win.
- ❖ If society isn't right, then fix it.
- ❖ A marble head fool has no place to lay his head.
- ❖ If someone wishes to engage you in a pissing contest, don't piss.
- ❖ If you are fortunate to accumulate great wealth, put it to great use.
- ❖ The things that challenge you the most may yield the greatest value.
- ❖ All sensible things are possible.
- ❖ If you expect the guru to have all the answers you may become disappointed.
- ❖ Praise and accolades can never equal extraordinary good deeds.
- ❖ If you are waiting for wisdom, don't hold your breath.
- ❖ If you sit on the bank long enough something is bound to bite your line.
- ❖ Do not judge others according to your weaknesses.
- ❖ Do not make assumptions based on ignorance and apply them to others.
- ❖ Do not consume more things than you can afford.
- ❖ Leadership is more than running your mouth.
- ❖ You can't change your past but you can chart your future.
- ❖ How can you help others less fortunate? What are your gifts and talents? Once you know the answers to these questions then figure out a way to assist. Changing lives for the better is one of the most important things human beings can do.

Jewels of Success

Why do some people succeed and others fail? I would imagine that question has been asked over one million times. I do not claim to have a complete answer to this question. However, I am prone to believe that mental attitude is a determining factor in whether you succeed or fail. I further believe that a person succeeds because he chooses a goal that is obtainable and follows a course of action that leads to the goal. On the contrary, a person who fails does the opposite.

Surely, this is a simplistic answer but one that has profound merit. I further maintain that success is doing the very best that you can after repeated trial and error in pursuit of your goal. Success is usually obtainable over periods of time. Failure is a stumbling block that can be overcome through knowledge, skill, experience, time and ability. For example, I recall learning to ride a bike. I would watch my older brothers and neighbors ride bicycles with ease. I desired to learn because it seemed like fun. I would try and try without much success at first. I would fall after wobbling a short distance. I was encouraged to keep trying and turning in the direction I was falling. After several weeks of trial and error, I lost fears, gained confidence and learned to ride a bike.

The pearls of wisdom below may be helpful to anyone who desires to achieve any goal in life.

- The key to success is having the right people doing the right things at the right time.
- The road to success is not as easy as it appears.
- Spend your time wisely. Do not dwell on trivia.
- The mind must be exercised to accomplish any goal.
- Success requires constant struggle and change.
- If you do your best, shame will not follow your trail.
- Winners are propelled by motivation.
- Motivation is the pathway to success.
- Losers are driven by appetite.
- Drive is more valuable than intelligence in the quest for success.
- Modesty will get you nowhere fast.
- Persistence is the key to achievement.
- Success is earned. No one will give it to you.
- Stop daydreaming of success and make it happen.
- Success is achieved through trial, error, hard work and failure.
- Do not be afraid to fail. Do not be afraid to take risks. You will not succeed if you do not try.
- Do not seek failure. Never let it trap you. But, if it crosses your path, do not be afraid.
- Always use failure as a learning experience and where possible as a stepping stone.
- Success is a personal journey full of faith, ambition, conviction, common sense and realization.
- You must realize which pathway leads to success.
- Success is a relatively small achievement for some and an extraordinary accomplishment for others.
- Success exists at different levels.
- Be patient and move along as your goal becomes closer.
- Do not worry whether you succeed or fail. Do your best and let the chips fall where they may.

- ❖ Success carries a high premium in some cases.
- ❖ Success may not fall into your lap but if you are prepared it will be within your grasp.
- ❖ Success may not be recognizable at first glance.
- ❖ If you must be successful, go after it with great fortitude.
- ❖ Success builds up over time. It does not happen overnight.
- ❖ Success is peace of mind.
- ❖ Do not allow others to chose your brand of success.
- ❖ Success is innate.
- ❖ Success marks the high points in life.
- ❖ Success is part of all you do.
- ❖ Everyone has the potential to succeed.
- ❖ Success is not the appearance of things, but rather the substance of things achieved.
- ❖ If you are successful without fame someday public recognition will notice your achievements.
- ❖ Trial and tribulation build character.
- ❖ Every successful person has ups and downs.
- ❖ The great tragedy of failure is not defeat per se but the lamenting, self-doubting and self-pitting surrounding it. These are the real dangers.
- ❖ Success is whatever failure is not.
- ❖ There are many reasons for failure but few for success.
- ❖ Do more things that reduce your failure rate.
- ❖ Success is yours to conquer.
- ❖ Success is there for you to behold.
- ❖ Success is a state of mind.
- ❖ Identify the things that will hinder you from accomplishing your goal. Eliminate them and find success.
- ❖ Victories are hollow achievements if they are unfairly attained or not appropriately celebrated.
- ❖ If you are going to do something well, you have to do it.

- ❖ A crook enjoys success until caught.
- ❖ Every day you try, you make progress.
- ❖ If you are waiting for discovery, you have already failed in your pursuits.
- ❖ If you are not winning, try something different.
- ❖ Never close a deal of which you have reservations. Persuade the dealmaker to meet your terms.
- ❖ As long as there is life there is opportunity to succeed.

Art of Philosophy

The most profound question of the day may be the simplest one. Why life? In other words, why do living creatures exist? Who or what is behind this grand scheme? The essence of this question gives birth to other questions. If you answer this question you unlock why human species is here and perhaps how we got here. The origin of all living creatures or beings began at some point. The mystery of which has mused generations throughout the annals of time. Absent knowledge of the beginning for the living renders many important questions inconclusive. Things known and speculated about the origins of the living span the gamut from creationism to big bang theory to evolutionism to pure fiction.

However, there is no definitive answer to this simple question. Maybe, the question is not so simple after all. If we proffer a hypothesis that all living creatures and beings self create then what conditions cause the creations and what originates these phenomena? I offer a theory of the unknown as a construct of knowledge that we yet understand. We are far more ignorant than we think. The unknown vastly outweighs what we know or even what we are capable of knowing. There are knowns and unknowns. Knowns are things we know. This means that our conscious mind is aware that they exist. These include obvious things, persons and places. For example, airplanes, people and cities can be realized through our senses. Unknowns are those not detected by our conscious minds. We are simply unaware of their existence. Even if we know of their existence through our unconscious or subconscious mind for all practical purposes they do not exist. These include the beginning and ending of time, order of nature, purpose of life and death and heaven and hell. These may not be realized through our senses. They are not temporal or celestial. They are ethereal.

Knowns are also what we know but unaware that we know. These are known as instincts, primal or gut level feelings and emotions. These may be considered coded in our DNA. For example, we instinctively know that fire burns, food nourishes, animals bite, parents are protectors, and foul odor harms. Human infants know these things but are unaware that they know them. Unknowns also include those we don't know that we don't know. These express our degrees of ignorance. They are bound by discovery and knowledge.

There is exponentially more to know than we know that exposes the vastness of our ignorance. It may not be possible to know all. Our human brain capacity is finite. The vastness of the world of the unknown is infinite. The volumes of knowledge that we acquire regardless of attainment merely scratches the surface. Our degrees of knowledge are miniscule relative to the unknown. What we don't know is mind-boggling? However, what we don't know that we don't know makes us appear successful. How great are the depth, breadth and length of our ignorance? The more we know, the more we know what we don't know. Those who are curious attempt to discover what they don't know. Through discovery comes advancement that allows successors to build on the foundation of predecessors. So, a little more of the unknown is made known. If things are well ordered, each succeeding generation uncovers more space of the unknown and reduces the gap between the known and unknown.

Our body of knowledge that is positive or provable is miniscule compared to the unknown world. There are unknowns that could unlock our most profound mysteries or questions. We have proven to some degree that we can solve some problems like configuring materials and manipulating chemicals to cause a machine to move or fly, or to develop tools and devices to repair human bones and tissues or treat and cure some illnesses. We have also manipulated micro materials to create devices for transmitting signals and data for academic, leisure and business purposes. We have even discovered therapies and chemicals to enhance our human bodies. These things provide evidence that some among us are capable of figuring out some things in the unknown universe.

However, the degrees of ignorance among us modulate how fast we advance as a civilization and simultaneously prohibit us from discovering the vastness of the unknown. This is the challenge to our generation-finding ways of accelerating knowledge and decelerating ignorance. If knowledge can be produced at a greater pace than ignorance and consumed at that rate then civilization will accelerate at greater speed. The darkness of the unknown world will reduce proportionately when that happens.

- ❖ Every person has the same basic needs and desires. Differences among persons happen through time, environment and circumstances.
- ❖ Consumer behavior is driven by appetite.
- ❖ Orchestrated noise is music.
- ❖ Music is organized noise.
- ❖ Singing is slurred speech.
- ❖ Creativity is the genius of the soul.
- ❖ Prophecy is tomorrow's dream. Wisdom is yesterday's gift. Knowledge is the future's promise.
- ❖ Society is a coconut.
- ❖ Culture is a matter of preference.
- ❖ Reality is timely. Death is timeless.
- ❖ Greatness cannot be suppressed.
- ❖ Philosophy is a leisure exploration of the mind.
- ❖ Pure thought blossoms like spring flowers.

- ❖ Human beings are basically equal regardless of social status.
- ❖ Human beings are basically the same regardless of physical appearance.
- ❖ Race is not a significant factor of intelligence. There are exceptions in all racial groups. Each group spans the intelligence continuum. Each group has its fair share of geniuses, prodigies, and idiots.
- ❖ Racism will exist as long as there are racial differences.
- ❖ Race matters only to a racist.
- ❖ Human beings are more relaxed with people, places and things from their subculture.
- ❖ The glass ceiling has turned into stone.
- ❖ Share the fruits of your labor and find peace of mind.
- ❖ An individual never repeats the same thing precisely.
- ❖ Money is evil. It spoils those with it and tortures those without it.
- ❖ In spite of its miraculous ability, the mind is not perfect.
- ❖ Everyone is ignorant-some greater than others.
- ❖ Nothing is more painful for a thinking person than constant boredom.
- ❖ Nothing is more boring than routine trivia.
- ❖ Sameness creates a dull life.
- ❖ Society keeps functioning after you are gone.
- ❖ Human beings are composites of their environment.
- ❖ Human beings are confined by their physical environment; They escape through their mental capacities.
- ❖ Everyone lives in a realm of reality. Destiny is determined by interpretation of it.
- ❖ The mind is human beings' greatest asset; without it their environment becomes meaningless.
- ❖ The human mind is our best friend and worst enemy.
- ❖ A mind is set in motion by thinking.

- The mind is a storehouse of truth. Seek and find the answers.
- The mind is a sea of thoughts. Fish deeply for the rare ones.
- The mind is absent of matter and capable of comprehending all.
- Small minds wander between narrow spaces.
- A person is no more than thought, being and action.
- An empty head holds little promise.
- A free mind is a necessity.
- Creativity demands freedom of thought.
- You know it is time to change jobs when you become embarrassed to say what you do for a living.
- There is peace and tranquility in meditation, reading and writing.
- It is not the school that makes the grade but rather the student.
- Too much debt may rob you of your principles.
- What happens to an artist without a canvas on which to express ideas? The artist expresses nothing at all or finds another medium.
- Learn all you can while young. As you grow older you will amass a fortune of knowledge.
- No asylum can contain a restless soul.
- If a business venture is worthwhile, it will generate demand.
- If you produce something of great value demand will follow.
- Search for the good in people.
- Everyone is young until age catches up.
- The absence of common sense is a curse.
- Genius is not created or manipulated by force. It is natural.
- If you screen friends too carefully, you are likely to end with none.
- One common factor among humankind is degree of ignorance.
- Change the world one thought after another, one day at a time.
- The student doesn't learn everything in school. A great deal of knowledge and skills are acquired in other places.
- If our government is running amuck abroad, what should we expect at home?

- The laughter of a fool is as great as his level of ignorance.
- Liberty cannot be achieved in civilized society but rather only varying degrees of restraint.
- The great imbalance of wealth in the world will always burden those with it to pursue equal or greater measures of power.
- Did the caveman seek a better life or was he content with life? Is post-modern person better off than her cave dwelling ancestors? How did the caveman solve pressing problems? Did he use instinct, mystics or logic?
- Things of the heart do matter and special attention should be devoted to them. Deprivation of the needs of the heart will cause great pain.
- We acquire knowledge not for its sake only, nor for our gratification only, but for the greater good of humankind.
- As a social scientist, I see things with a skeptic's eye. That's not necessarily cynical, but more or less cautious and observant about what is occurring or not, and not being spellbound by the pageantry.
- The soul of a person determines character.
- If you are looking for trouble, you will not have difficulty finding it.
- Every goon or loon has his or her moments.
- What is the true world history?
- The one who lies is likely to entrap himself.
- If all of the low hanging fruit is gone, either climb the tree or shake it.
- I catch thoughts much like a fisherman or outfielder.
- An unjust law should always be challenged in order to bring forth justice.
- People who are shortsighted might consider themselves visionaries.
- The best place to find justice is where government is affirmed by the people.

❖ Facts don't lie; truth is constant.

❖ If you are not seeking fame and fortune, what are you doing?

❖ There is nothing more ridiculous than a compassionate fool.

❖ The trivia you pursue will always be extra baggage.

❖ Hypocrites will be the first to charge you with all of their guilt and failures.

❖ The problem with ignorance is that those who suffer from it are often unaware of its effects.

Overtures of Politics

Politics is the power people exercise to influence or sway others to adopt, accept, or submit to their way. This power may operationalize on a *personal*, *group*, or *mass* level. For example, two people hold a conversation about their relationship. One asserts that we have known one another for 10 years but have not once expressed how fortunate we are to know one another. The other replies perhaps that's a good thing because if we truly expressed our relationship with one another we may increase its risk of falling apart.

The first person responds that I am certain the relationship will not dissolve because our bonds are pliable and durable. I cannot imagine anything that could be said or done that would break up the relationship. The other quips we have nothing in common. We are political opposites. I am liberal and you are conservative. I am an extrovert and you are an introvert. I like name brand everything and you are satisfied with generic brands. I like living with pets and you can't stand being around them anymore. I enjoy hunting and fishing. You do not. Yet in spite of our differences, we can work together to block a recycling plant from locating in our community. Will you join me in a NIMBY campaign? Yes, I will. I always trust your judgment in all things political.

Politics is about power and relationships. It also is about influence. It is about allocation of resources. A group of neighbors meet to decide what to do with a $10,000 allocation they received from City Hall for neighborhood welfare and improvements. One faction wants to have a block party, another wants to erect a fence, yet another wants to use it as a benevolent fund. Faction one argues that we need to get to know our neighbors better and the best way to do that is to have one big block party with food, activities, and music. We get to interact informally with one another and that will make for better community. Faction two states that that's OK but it's a one-time event that will not have lasting effect. Everyone may have fun but eventually the money would be all gone and we would be right back to square one. So if we put up a fence across the vacant lot where transients make a short cut through our neighborhood that would benefit the entire neighborhood. Transients would not pass through our neighborhood and we would all feel safer about our kids playing in their yards and elders would not feel threaten by strangers strolling through.

The third faction asserts that all of what has been said is good and true but if we really want to build community what better way to do that than providing financial assistance to a neighbor in need. We have a significant number of retirees in the neighborhood living on fixed income and their income may not be sufficient if there is a health emergency, death of a spouse, or major property damage loss, or even a high utility bill. If we establish a benevolent fund, we would be able to assist our neighbors in need. Doing so would be the best use of the $10,000 allocation. The neighbors decide on one of the three options.

On a mass level, politics is at play in many ways however I focus on one here. A group of legislators have proposed a referendum to legalize marijuana in their state. Their primary argument is that it's on the streets and "pushers" are selling it through the black market so why not legalize and tax it and redirect law enforcement's resources elsewhere. Opponents argue that it goes against our morals and legalizing the sale of marijuana adds yet another sanctioned sin into society. More "pot-heads" will be on the streets and highways creating accidents, mayhem, and mischief. The measure floats through the House and Senate and the governor approves it as a state referendum to be placed on the next ballot. The people decide. In all of the cases above there is a decision to be made. So, politics ultimately is about making decisions, influence, relationships, allocation of resources and power.

- ❖ The question is not whether a majority rule is better than minority rule or single rule, but whether a majority should rule in a just society. The majority of citizens in a democratic regime should govern even if their collective decisions are wrong, detrimental, or otherwise not beneficial to society at large. Arguably, in a republic, a majority has absolute authority to error or make just and profitable decisions.
- ❖ As is the case in a tyrannical regime, an individual exercises absolute power and control and executes good and bad decisions. Therefore, the form of governance is not the issue and not about what authority one or the other possesses but about justice. All three forms of government can bring about justice however majority rule is more likely to do so than the others. This appears to be true because a majority has the propensity to represent public will.
- ❖ If there were no citizens, there would be no need for politicians, bureaucrats or governments.
- ❖ Integrity must be earned. It cannot be bought or stolen.
- ❖ Although everyone is affected by it, everyone cannot lead.
- ❖ Some people should never be entrusted with power.
- ❖ A typical committee meeting is not worth a hill of beans.
- ❖ One indicator of a good administrator is how well he gets monkeys of his back.
- ❖ Administrators with little ambition also have little motivation.
- ❖ A person with little ambition has little motivation to excel.
- ❖ A person who is predictable brings little to the table of negotiation.
- ❖ People are inconsiderate of others because they are too consumed with themselves.

- ❖ Poor people in capitalistic society cannot achieve parity with the ruling class if they do not have equal opportunity to generate wealth.
- ❖ While providing food, clothing and shelter may sustain poor people, these things alone are not enough to lift them out of poverty.
- ❖ Until poor people are able to fend for themselves in a free and open economy they will remain trap in the cycle of poverty.
- ❖ Society discourages ambition and stifles creativity.
- ❖ Peace neutralizes turmoil.
- ❖ Financial independence is a prerequisite in today's capitalistic democracy.
- ❖ Treat your foes with kindness even though they may barrage you with hostility.
- ❖ An ally will do as much for you as you do for the ally.
- ❖ A cause is worth more than fame or fortune.
- ❖ Every problem can be solved. Nothing is invincible.
- ❖ Human beings are their worst enemy. They are responsible for their actions and consequences.
- ❖ Plant seeds wherever you go. You may have to travel that road again.
- ❖ There is an appetite for greatness that separates martyrs from ordinary men.
- ❖ It is quite ironic that persons with authority are not looking for leaders to fill key vacancies but rather followers.
- ❖ People are easily deceived by the appearance of things.
- ❖ People are like plants; some develop naturally and others need cultivation.
- ❖ Be sure of yourself before exploring the unknown.
- ❖ Always reach out and help those less fortunate and expect nothing in return.
- ❖ If you cannot soar with the eagle, run with the quail.

- Depend upon no one except yourself.
- It is not necessary to wear a crown.
- Every argument is not yours to hold.
- Do not expect to be showered with praise for standing up for righteousness but to be hailed with scorn.
- In a world of imperfect beings, the ideal is not possible.
- Institutions are not built for the individual but rather for individuals.
- It is much easier to replace individuals than institutions.
- People find fault in little things after they have failed to do so with big ones.
- Where there is a bad crop of leaders, rot rises to the top.
- Do not worry whether those who despise you will hinder your progress. Keep forging ahead.
- Your decisions determine whether you will land in the valley of failure or on the mountaintop of victory.
- Do not harbor blind ambition.
- Do not allow ambition to run away from your ability. Bridle it.
- Your turn is whenever you decide to move.
- Stop waiting for the right opportunity. Make it.
- Do not accept anyone's solution unless you are convinced it will work for you.
- Do not take risks unless you can afford to pay the price for failure.
- Never accept no as the final answer when you fall short of your goal.
- If you can bear any pain, shoulder any burden, and face any challenge, you possess the capacity for greatness.
- Follow the path that leads to your goal.
- Pay little attention to naysayers.
- Do not expect a helping hand but it reaches out to you grab it.

- People who have formed an opinion of you may control your upward mobility.
- Absorb all of the blows that land on you and persevere.
- It is a rare breed that breaks away from the pack.
- Do not be afraid to press your luck. Take it to the outer limits.
- If you do not have a plan, you do not have a commitment. If you do not achieve desired results, you do not have a sufficient plan or commitment.
- Take every task as you find it and mold it into something you like.
- The true measure of a moral leader is how well she deploys her power for good.
- A politician is not bound by what he says but by what he does.
- In a political fight, who wins the infantile giant or the whining small person?
- In all things political every winner compromises.
- Straw men, paper tigers and puppets prefer political theater.
- Immigration policy ought to be fair and impartial and not subject to political whim.
- The political stooge who runs for public office deserves a public whipping.
- The political aims of a nation should never be personal.
- A narcissistic political leader will become tyrannical once he has acquired enough power.
- In ordinary society, ordinary people become elected officials.
- In fair elections, the right to vote reigns; in corrupt elections, authority rules.
- What kind of leader rules in a village of idiots?
- Why does evil leadership appear more frequently in some states than others?
- If the body politic is cancerous, why expect it policies to be healthy?

- ❖ No person should encroach on the rights of another without good reason; nor should any nation interfere with or intrude into the affairs of another without just cause.
- ❖ The political atrocities that nations engage in today are abominations against humanity.
- ❖ If the political actor in you convinces you that injustice is good then the show is over.
- ❖ The way to stop a politician or elected official from attaining personal gain is to strip him or her of authority.
- ❖ It amazes me how hard some politicians work to do wrong.
- ❖ The way you enter into a meeting determines how you come out.
- ❖ How can there be political equality in a capitalistic society?

About the Book

This book is about the challenges, hopes and dreams that people grapple with everyday. It is a book of rich thoughts on being young, spirituality, hope, success, philosophy, and politics. It is rife with common sense and inspiration. This masterful work has been in creative process since the late 1970s. A must read for every generation.

About the Author

Dr. Ray C. Minor is a program officer and scholar at the Kettering Foundation. He has extensive executive and management experience in public, private, and nonprofit sectors. Minor's research interests include citizen participation and engagement, democracy, public authorities and institutions, and nongovernmental organizations. Dr. Minor served in the Governor's Cabinet in Alabama and held cabinet posts at a major nonprofit in New Jersey and two liberal arts colleges in Alabama and Texas. He was founding President and Chairman Emeritus of the David Mathews Center for Civic Life. Dr. Minor graduated from the University of Alabama with a Bachelor of Science in Social Welfare and a Master in Higher Education Administration. He earned a Ph.D. in Public Policy and Administration from Walden University. Dr. Minor was co-editor of *Beyond Politics as Usual: Paths for Engaging College Students in Politics* (2017). He was author of *Reflections on President Barack Obama. The First President of Color of the United States* (2018) and *Donald J. Trump. The Tyrant in the White House* (2019). He is the author of *Democratic Citizenship and Public Administration. Democratic Arrangements and Democratic Practices.* (Expected publishing date 2020).

www.ingramcontent.com/pod-product-compliance
Lightning Source LLC
Chambersburg PA
CBHW050707250726
48662CB00002B/882